FIT *for* SERVICE

Recycle Inefficiency into Philanthropy

DAVID CHILDS, PhD

TATE PUBLISHING & *Enterprises*

TATE PUBLISHING
& *Enterprises*

Tate Publishing is committed to excellence in the publishing industry. Our staff of highly trained professionals, including editors, graphic designers, and marketing personnel, work together to produce the very finest books available. The company reflects the philosophy established by the founders, based on Psalms 68:11,

"THE LORD GAVE THE WORD AND GREAT WAS THE COMPANY OF THOSE WHO PUBLISHED IT."

If you would like further information, please contact us:

1.888.361.9473 | www.tatepublishing.com

TATE PUBLISHING & *Enterprises*, LLC | 127 E. Trade Center Terrace Mustang, Oklahoma 73064 USA

Fit for Service: Recycle Inefficiency into Philanthropy

Cover design by Melanie Harr-Hughes
Interior design by Lynly Taylor

Published in the United States of America

ISBN: 978-1-5988666-3-6

06.02.13

DEDICATION

Fit For Service is dedicated first to God. Ten years ago I lay in a hospital emergency room, being told that they would get me to the next available operating table if I remained alive until one became available. Since that night, my "second" life has been dedicated to the purpose for which God kept me alive, this book and its mission of "recycling inefficiency into philanthropy."

Secondly, I dedicate *Fit For Service* to my wife, Alice Canham, and my daughters, Lauren Elaine and Emily Claire. They personify, for me, God's will that we live with love and joy. And I hope *Fit For Service* will be a lasting reminder to them of who I am, what God put me here to do, and that I did it.

ACKNOWLEDGEMENTS

I first want to thank God for assigning to me such a wonderful, joyful and fulfilling life's mission.

Secondly, I want to thank my wife, Alice Canham, and my daughters, Lauren Elaine and Emily Claire, for being living reminders of God's love, joy and zest for life.

Third, I want to acknowledge those people who have been the compasses of my life's intended path: 1) my parents and grandparents, who gave me my values; 2) Dottie Thompson, Marvin Thomas and Earl Bullock, who gave me a career;

3) Steve Weimar, Grace Christiphine and Jeannette Sledge who gave me an extended family.

Fourth, I want to acknowledge those who typed, proofed, edited and advised during the creation of *Fit For Service:* Alice Canham, Emily Childs, Grace Christiphine, Jeannette Sledge, Darlene Beck and Linda Van Sant.

All of you have made *Fit For Service* both possible and what it is.

"He has erected a multitude of new offices, and sent hither swarms of officers to harass our people and eat out their substance."

"The high corporate mortality rate seems unnatural. No living species suffers from such a discrepancy between its maximum life expectancy and the average span it realizes. Why do so many companies die young? Companies die because their managers focus exclusively on producing goods and services and forget that the organization is a community of human beings that is in the business—any business—to stay alive."

TABLE OF CONTENTS

The Confession

We all know that self-improvement 12-Step programs begin with a confession—an admission that we have a problem. And so it is with this program.

And we also know that first step is often the most intimidating and difficult. So, let's take a deep breath, take that first step together and get started.

Okay, if it helps, I'll go first.

"My name is David Childs and I am a drone."

There. Now it's your turn.

"My name is _____ and I am a drone."

Congratulations! You said it—just blurted it right out! Now the hardest part is over and we can move on with the rest of the journey towards becoming a happy, healthy, productive member of an energized, actualized organization.

The Calling

Another exercise that is often utilized in self-help programs is known as the "sharing", the reflective life story of how one came to be sitting in this 12-Step circle on a Tuesday night.

For me, I started down my long sordid path in 1983 when I took a job as a manager in a bureaucratic organization. Of course, I had heard all the stories, allegations, and complaints about bureaucratic mismanagement and ineptitude that are a major part of urban folklore and media headlines. And, in the back of my mind, I had made a mental note to make sure that I became a bit of a crusader against any waste or managerial silliness that I might encounter. Never did I expect that I would be deluged with unimaginable ridiculousness from the very moment that I walked into the room.

On the morning of my first day, as I took my initiation

tour, I stopped behind one employee and tried to determine the subject matter and purpose of the form she was completing. As I analyzed the form, I noticed that she had typed (1983 was still the era of typewriters) the same name into six different blanks. My curiosity was piqued:

"Excuse me. Do you always type the same name into all six blanks, or do you sometimes enter different names?"

"No, it's always the same name."

"Is there some legal reason that the form must be designed that way or phrased that way?"

"No, not that I am aware of."

"How many of these forms do you fill out each day?"

"Oh, probably about two hundred."

"May I have a couple of the forms, please?"

I took the forms to my desk, left the first blank empty so that the name could be typed in, but replaced the remaining five blanks with the phrase "the above-named". I presented the modified form to the employee for her approval and then made an additional 500 copies for her. She thanked me and resumed her task—a task that had just been reduced by 83 percent!

I was hooked. I moved from her desk to another, seeking more opportunities to implement efficiencies.

Today I am still hooked; still looking; and still finding.

The Obstacles

After several months of looking for, finding and improving a multitude of procedures in my workplace, while also learning immensely more about bureaucratic culture and environment, I began to identify some of the ingrained bureaucratic perceptions, proverbs and procedures that foster, incubate and enable inefficiency.

You are probably already familiar with, and tortured by, many of them: the assembly line (cogs in the wheel) self-image, the myopic dedication to assembly line procedure, the sanctity of the proverb "if it ain't broke, don't fix it" because fixing it or even tweaking it can only be done at the price of interfering with, even stopping, production.

Yet, I also noticed that the bureaucratic assembly line was not completely scientific, mechanized, and/or sterile. It was also dramatically influenced by human behavior: laziness, alliances, favoritism, self-serving decision-making.

This insight caused me to realize that an organization is not a sterile, inert bureaucratic mechanized assembly line, because it is far too impacted by human behavior. It is, instead, a living, changing, teeming mass of human and mechanical cells that combine to form a living organism.

This was the "ah-hah" moment, the instant of epiphany and enlightenment; for once I realized that an organization is not a bureaucracy, but an organism, then all the other pieces began to fall into place.

The Right Question

The greatest piece of academic wisdom that I ever heard in a classroom occurred when a professor rephrased a student's question, then advised that the most critical step toward enlightenment is to ask the right question. For if you do not ask the right question, then all of the ensuing search for truth has been directed down an invalid path.

And so it was with my "ah-hah" moment. I realized that I had been asking the wrong questions regarding how to improve efficiency. I had simply accepted the description of my organization as a bureaucratic assembly line that was infected with negative, unmotivated people. That false premise led me to ask false questions ("How do you fine tune or dramatically improve the processes of an assembly line without seriously impacting production?" "How do you get negative people to stop being negative?"); and, consequently, to pursue false answers.

When I realized that my organization was not a robotic bureaucracy but a living organism, my entire perspective changed, causing the questions to change. "How do you tweak a process?" became "How do you make the organism happier, healthier, more productive?" "How do you combat negativity?" became "What are the ways to give people purpose?"

In short, the fundamental, core perspective and question changed from "How do I fix a broken piece of robotic bureaucracy?" to "How do I make this living organization healthier?"

The Right Answer

Once I realized that my organization was a living organism, I began to recognize parallels between the structures of organisms and organizations. Both have brain/nervous systems, both have musculoskeletal foundations, both have joints, both express themselves with "body language", both need to control their "bad cholesterol" count. Altogether, I have identified at least 12 parallels between organisms and organizations. (There are undoubtedly more to be discovered as this new field of study becomes more sophisticated.)

It is generally agreed among doctors, psychologists, health experts, etc. that there are three interdependent elements to a successful health plan for organisms: diet, exercise and esteem. The truly, completely healthy organism focuses on and constantly brings these three elements into ever stronger, healthier harmony.

Consequently, a theory of how to make a bureaucracy more efficient, er, uh, that is make an organization healthier, began to evolve. It became clear that just as you improve an organism's health by subjecting its component parts to a regimen of diet, exercise and esteem; you could improve an organization's health, efficiency and performance by doing exactly the same thing.

With that insight, I began looking for the elements of my organization that were not unique to it, but generic to all organizations. I began to analyze not only how to improve Form 31-U specifically, but how to improve "Forms" in general; how to make "Forms" healthier through a regimen of diet, exercise and esteem.

It was a "Eureka" moment! My organization was a living organism. And my organization had universal attributes (forms, signs, computers, telephones) just like organisms do (eyes, legs, muscles, hormones). And my organization could be made healthier by subjecting its universal component parts to a regimen of diet, exercise, and esteem, just like an organism.

Since that "Eureka" moment, the past twenty years have been dedicated to identifying those universal component parts and developing a regimen of diet, exercise and esteem for each of them.

At this point, it is appropriate to make a few key points:

- This plan was not created in a sanitized, out-of-touch academic laboratory. It was developed in a real, functioning bureaucratic organization by real department managers grappling with real world employees, customers, rules, budgets and challenges.

- Not only was it developed in the real world, by real people, in a real organization; it has also been designed to be "do-able" in a real world bureaucratic environment. Just as the most effective long-term health regimens are those that become part of our daily lifestyle (taking X supplements each morning, eating Y in the car on the way to work, working out at Z time every other day); so it is with this plan. It is designed to become part of the routine "daily life" of your organization.

- Just as you can measure your personal improvement in health by monitoring weight loss, checking body fat ratios, increasing treadmill levels and smiling

more, this plan tells you how to monitor
and measure your organization's health.

So, if an organization's health can be measured, have I actually done it? Have I monitored and measured the impact of the 12-Step Fitness Plan on various organizations? Does this 12-Step Fitness Plan for Organizations really work?

6

The Results

Yes, the plan works; and spectacularly.

Over the past twenty years, the Actualized Organization 12-Step Fitness Plan has been implemented in two organizations; one for six years and one for seventeen. The "Results" chart speaks for itself:

ACTUALIZED ORGANIZATION 12-STEP FITNESS PLAN RESULTS

Organization	Period	# Of Staff	Budget Growth	Recognition
Actualized Organization #1	1983 - 89	161 to 158	68%	3 National Awards
Equivalent Organization (No Fitness Plan)	1983 - 89	184 to 237	158.4%	None
Actualized Organization #2	1989 - 2006	230 to 224	27%	3 State Awards 4 National Awards

Actualized Organization #2 performs two specific functions. In one function it has a higher "widgets produced per staff member" efficiency ratio than any other such organization in its State, and is producing 181 percent more widgets than 15 years ago with exactly the same number of staff.

The second function has the highest "widget per staff" efficiency ratio of any comparable office in the entire nation; and production has doubled while staff has declined by 33 percent.

Organization #2
Strength and Fitness Measures—1989 to 2006

Function (Work-out Station)	# Of Staff (Height/Weight)	Widgets produced (Machine Weight Amount/Reps; Treadmill Speed/Incline)
#1	Same	181 % Increase
#2	33% Less	100 % Increase

Not only has Organization #2 dramatically improved its strength and fitness, but it has also significantly boosted its self-esteem. Fifteen years ago it was an organization that no one wanted to be around. Employees did not want to come to work. The organization was flooded with customer complaints. When I first joined the organization, one of my first functions was to develop a Customer Apology Form letter, and I averaged sending out 8 to 10 per day!

Today, fifteen years later, I am complimented an average of once a day by someone saying that our organization is the finest of its type that the customer has ever experienced. Our business has increased nationwide because customers seek-out our dedication, sincerity, integrity and efficiency. Last year, one-third of our staff received a written "Thank You" letter for their quality of service.

When I first joined the organization fifteen years ago, my goal was for it to simply become competent. Today, I am stunned that it has become not merely competent, but documentably one of the finest organizations of its kind in the nation. In human terms, the 12-Step Fitness Plan has transformed my organization from a depressed, out of shape hypochondriac into a happy, confident actualized organism.

We all know how to get healthier: develop a daily routine that includes a healthy diet, regular exercise, and positive vibes. Then, stick with it.

The 12-Step Fitness Plan does just that. It builds diet, exercise and esteem affirmations into the daily routine of your organization. Do it! Your staff, customers, stockholders, banker, and family will be glad you did.

7

Nature: *An* Organization's Soul

(Office Environment)

THE PURPOSEFUL FAMILY

We all know that the core key element of a healthy, happy, successful lifestyle is attitude. As it relates to people, psychologists refer to the importance of nature, of environment, in shaping attitudes and perceptions. Studies show that newborns tend to inherit depression from their mother, for example. Babies of drug addicts are often born with the addiction.

An organization's daily operating environment is, equally, the foundation, the cornerstone for obstacles or opportunities, failures or successes. Organizational leadership analysts like Deming, Herzberg, Maslow and McGregor consistently state that productivity improves as an office creates a more humane, ethical, purposeful environment—an environment where employees not only understand the big picture mission and their own unique function in it, but also feel a part of the organization and are appreciated for their contributions to it. This is known as a "purposeful family" environment, where mission, purpose, civility, humanity and teamwork create success.

As just stated, an immense amount has been written about how to create the successful organizational environment. The simplest way that I have found to summarize, condense and be able to remember the key components of a "purposeful family" environment is to let the acronym "TAP into CCHI" become your mantra.

First, the mantra has meaning. TAP-ing into your organization's CCHI means that your mission is to develop and unleash your organization's positive energy to successfully accomplish its mission.

Second, the acronym of the mantra reminds you of the individual elements that must be present to create the "purposeful family" environment; to unleash your organization's full energy and potential:

Tradition	(Pride)		Creativity
Atmosphere	(CCHI)	*into your organization's*	Civility
Purpose	(Mission,		Humanity
	Goals)		Integrity

Tradition (Pride)—Individuals and families take pride in who they are, where they came from, and their accomplishments. Families keep old photographs, put their children's honors on display, have family reunions and take pride in the first family member graduating from college.

So should organizations. Many quality organizations display historical photos of old offices or previous staffs, display a Hall of Fame of Outstanding Employees, initiate new employees with films of the organization's illustrious history, wear Organization Logo shirts, have Organization picnics, display awards, or exhibit innumerable other manifestations of history, tradition, unity and pride.

Atmosphere (CCHI)—A person's aura, image and vibes emanate from their attitude, their essence, their soul, their chi. And much of a person's chi is formed by the family chi that they grew up in. The same is true for the atmosphere, the CCHI of your office. We will discuss this in more detail in a couple of paragraphs.

Purpose (Mission, Goals)—Some of the most pivotal moments in our lives occur when we are given purpose: the moment that we realize what we want our career to be, the moment that we meet the love of our life. A clearly defined and understood purpose is just as critical to an organization as to an individual or family, and the organization's purpose must constantly be clearly defined, communicated, monitored and re-enforced.

CCHI is central to the Purposeful Family environment that you are trying to foster. An office's atmosphere, its chi, permeates the attitudes of employees, the decision-making process, the establishing of priorities, the determination of cost-benefits, the office's self-image; literally every element of the office's essence.

A healthy organizational CCHI is maintained when the organization's atmosphere is composed of Civility, Creativity, Humanity, and Integrity.

A comparative study of world-wide philosophies/faiths reveals 10 universal truths that are repeatedly promoted:

Common Good	Love
Fairness–Justice	Participation–Empowerment
Honoring Commitments	Respect
Human Dignity	Social Responsibility/Philanthropy
Integrity	Truth

These truths can be summarized as Civility, Humanity and Integrity, and adherence to these Universal Principals creates CHI.

The additional C (creativity) is equally crucial, as it provides the vital link between Atmosphere and Purpose; for creativity will only emerge where it is desired, requested, promoted and honored. Repressive, dictatorial environments asphyxiate freedom, expression, and intellectual curiosity. Creativity can only survive and thrive in the incubation of CHI. The promotion and praising of creativity lends your workplace a lighter atmosphere; and the more joy in the workplace (hah-hah), the more opportunity for insight and inspiration (Ah-hahh)!

Quality organizations create the CHI that unleashes Creativity, which is then directed toward more effectively and efficiently achieving the organization's Purposes, goals and missions.

Again,

Tradition   (Pride)

Atmosphere   (CCHI)

Purpose   (Mission, Goals)

into your organization's

Creativity

Civility

Humanity

Integrity

and create the Purposeful Family.

Diet

As for developing a diet that promotes a healthy environment, the key mantra is "quality intake." Just as we put wholesome foods into our bodies to become healthier, an organization's health is dependent upon the intake of quality personnel, equipment, computer programs and ideas.

How one improves the health and quality of equipment, technology, forms and other parts of your organization will be detailed later. In this section, and the next one, we will focus on identifying quality "Natures" in personnel, then how to "Nurture" that "Nature".

In short, your organization wants to be composed of personnel/staff that are, as Abraham Maslow defined, actualizers. Actualizers are those who are happy with their own lives, content with their lifestyle. Freed from personal wants, needs, emotional baggage, they seek fulfillment by producing for and giving to others.

Of course, the first problem is that there aren't many such people. But by TAP-ing into your organization's CCHI, you have created the actualized environment that attracts them. So, the issue of "How does my organization attract them?" has already been solved!

The next question is "How do I know one of them when I see them in an interview?" A study of "actualized" quality organizations and their hiring practices reveals that there are certain traits ("PHACES") that quality organizations look for during an interview. Does the interviewee exhibit:

- **P** ositive, constructive, "half-full" outlook rather than a defeatist, can't do, "half-empty";

- **H** appy, positive, sense of humor;

- **A** lert, attentive, focused eyes, neither nervously darting nor lethargic or inattentive;

- **C** omfortable confidence, neither arrogant bombast or mousy insecurity;

- **E** nergy that is healthy, focused and productive; neither nervous hyperactivity nor lethargy;

- **S** ophistication and verbal fluency.

These attributes are just as vital to your organization's health as are skills, education and experience, for it is these traits that identify those "actualized" individuals that, when they become staff members, will provide your organization's CCHI, infusing it with the positive energy necessary to evolve, to grow through PHACES, to thrive. The PHACES Interview Analysis Sheet will help you focus on and identify these traits.

PHACES

INTERVIEW ANALYSIS SHEET

POSITIVE

Negative   Positive

Defeatist   Constructive

Can't Do   Let's Do

Comments: _____

HAPPY

Unhappy   Happy

Pessimistic   Humorous

Complainer

Blamer

Comments: _____

ALERT

Lethargic   Attentive

Inattentive   Focused

Distracted

Comments: _____

CONFIDENT

Insecure   Confident

Fearful   Relaxed

Arrogant   Understated

Comments: _____

ENERGETIC

Listless   Motivated

Discouraged   Purposeful

Hyper   Enthusiastic

Distracted

Comments: _____

SOPHISTICATED

Poor Communication   Fluent

Flawed Thought   Sound Reasoning

Crude Demeanor   Civility

Comments: _____

Exercise

The specific exercises that promote a stronger, healthier organization require you to personally: 1) walk through your organization; 2) ask about your employees, both their personal and professional condition; 3) empathize and/or facilitate solutions to problems and recognize/honor accomplishments and; 4) make sure that, at all times, you personify the image that you want the organization to project. You should personally symbolize the office's nature and image at all times, both within and outside of the organization. It is the equivalent of walking with ankle/wrist weights; in organizational terms you symbolize/project (walk) with an image/purpose (weights).

Esteem

Just as people have very distinct images (positive, negative, happy, depressive, manipulator, giver), so do organizations. You know of restaurant chains that consistently have more helpful wait staff than others, or airlines that treat you like people rather than cattle. Organizations have personalities, and those personalities (like human ones) are heavily impacted by the environment that incubates them.

So, what are some ways to project a positive environment

to let new employees know that they are being encouraged to TAP into and contribute to the organization's CCHI?

1. A professional Personnel/Human Resources Director/Department which, like yourself, personifies the nature, the attitude, the image that you want to permeate the organization. This person/department is a recruit's first, and consequently, most powerful impression of the organization's environment. Likewise, this person/department also has the task of not only outwardly projecting the organization's image, but of also screening applicants/recruits and making certain that the organization's intake of new employees will supply the organization with the necessary quality, healthy nutrients of CCHI and PHACES.

2. A quality personnel process (Recruiting, Interviewing, Hiring, Paperwork)—Just as the Personnel Director/Staff personify the image that your organization wishes to project, a new employee's experience with your hiring processes will tell them that you are serious not only about the quality of your image, but also about the quality of your processes. The recruiting, interviewing, hiring and paperwork processing experience should appear to the appli-

cant to be a quality, efficient "well-oiled machine."

The new employee has now been informed that you are committed to excellence both in image and in substance. Finally,

3. the organization welcomes the new member to the "Purposeful Family" by taking them on a personal tour of the organization, making them aware of functions, departments, organizational structure, bathrooms, and introducing them to the other employees.

A quality Personnel Department that recruits actualizers, processes them efficiently, and welcomes them warmly serves as the foundation for establishing and maintaining the organizational atmosphere of a "Purposeful Family" that exudes healthy, happy self-esteem.

REAL LIFE

The Vestibule of one organization prominently displays a huge banner that simply says "PIG!" When I asked its meaning, an employee recounted how it was from the Founder's favorite story about a man driving on a high, winding, dangerous mountain road. Suddenly, a young woman came swerving wildly around the bend, almost careening both of them off of the cliff. As she swerved by, inches away, she yelled "Pig!" The man, incensed, outraged at the disrespectful, dangerous young hoodlum yelled back at her "Sow!" Then, he rounded the bend and hit the pig. The Founder wanted this organization's staff to be helpful and caring; to yell "Pig!"

REAL LIFE

One organization's annual business cycle is such that one particular month is roughly three times as busy and hectic as the other months. The organization has named it "mint month" and the staff are provided unlimited mints both to lubricate their throats for a lot of sales talk, and just as a "pick me up." Management says that since "mint month" was instituted stamina, attitudes and sales remain strong the entire month whereas previously they would fade near the end of the month.

Such traditions can be critical cornerstones of organizational teamwork and pride.

Remember:

> Every Word You Speak,
> Every Behavior You Exhibit,
> Every Decision You Make,
> Personifies the Organization's Commitment to
> > TAP-ing into its CCHI.

Suggested Work-out Reminders

The Suggested Plan is a compilation of successful approaches that have been adopted by other organizations. It is intended to provide you with a list of successful programs that you may wish to implement as is, adapt, or use as suggestions to stimulate your own creative initiatives.

____ 1.   Select an office Environmentalist. Their function, for lack of a better term, is to be the organization's cheerleader. This person makes sure that things are done to create a positive, prideful atmosphere, that the healthy Purposeful Family environment is maintained, and conditions are maximized for TAP-ing into the organization's CCHI. The Environmentalist will probably want to participate in or supervise some of the following suggestions.

____ 2.   If your organization does not already recognize holidays, special fun days and/or the organization's significant historical events, the Environmentalist may wish to start making such days part of the organization's culture.

- Do you hunt plastic Easter eggs in the office for Easter?

- Do you have best carved pumpkin contests at Halloween?

- Do you have ugliest socks day?

- Do you honor the organization's founder's birthday or the anniversary of the big "breakthrough" contract?

____ 3. The Environmentalist may wish to form a committee whose purpose is to create, implement and maintain visibility for an organizational logo and mission statement. Both help create a foundation, pride and tradition.

____ 4. The Environmentalist may create a Tradition Committee to research, record and promote organizational great achievements, historic moments, folklore, Outstanding Employee Hall of Fame, etc.

____ 5. The Tradition Committee should create, maintain and update a Wall of Tradition.

____ 6. Produce a bi-monthly or quarterly organizational newsletter. The Newsletter might include:

- The Organization's logo

- Mission Statement

- Recent accomplishments, upgrades, improvements

- Procedure/law changes

- Reminders relative to correcting glitches

- Update on status of efforts to implement office goals

- Update on performance relative to performance standards

- Recognition of employees who have received an appreciation from a customer

- News from departments

- Employee profiles

- Recognition of birthdays, anniversaries, children, promotions, etc.

- Appropriate games, jokes, stories, etc.

- Any other relevant/appropriate contribution.

___ 7. Conduct quarterly meetings with representatives of the employees (The Employees' Congress) so that you can communicate with and learn from them directly.

___ 8. The Environmentalist should design, update and place in each new employee's packet a "Welcome to the Family" letter that includes a brief initiation into the Organization's history, lore, tradition, achievements and a welcome on becoming a part of it; signed by the Organization's President, the Human Resources Director, the Environmentalist, and the Chairman of the Tradition Committee.

___ 9. As a part of their first day, new hires should be given their "New Employee Packet" that includes not only the required rules, procedures, legal/tax forms, etc., but also the "Welcome to the Family" letter, a copy of the most recent Organization Newsletter, and the training materials for the department that they are assigned to. The Human Resources Director or the Environmentalist should take them on a tour of the Organization completed by a visit to and explanation of the Wall of Tradition.

Again, these are recommendations that have been consolidated and summarized from the multitude of successful concepts that quality organizations have implemented. They are provided as triggers/stimulators for the development of your own unique program that best TAPs into your organization's CCHI.

Nurture

(Development/Growth)

"Failure to Thrive" is the psychological phrase that applies to newborns and infants who are ignored and provided no mental, physical or emotional stimulation. The brain and muscles are not exercised, are given no stimulus to develop and, consequently, become lethargic, shrivel and die. Small trees that touch another tree or tall grass are stimulated and motivated to grow faster than trees that touch nothing. Organizations that become monopolies and are no longer stimulated by competition become inefficient, bloated and collapse.

Physical, mental and emotional growth depends upon stimulation and, obviously, the more constructive the stimulation, the more positive the results. Human and organizational development literature consistently discusses seven key contributors to healthy growth; or, if you will, there are 7 PHACES of Growth in healthy, thriving organizations:

7 PHACES OF GROWTH

- Hire
- Train
- Count
- Develop
- Encourage/Empower
- Constructively Discipline
- Reward

And, as no surprise to anyone, we find that these 7 necessary PHACES for growth comprise the necessary elements of diet, exercise and esteem needed to successfully NURTURE the Healthy Organization.

Diet

The Healthy Organization, just like a healthy person, intakes healthy nutrients and counts the amount of intake. It intakes healthy nutrients by hiring as many PHACES as possible. Again, PHACES are those who bring into the organization the nutrients of being Positive, Happy, Alert, Confident, Energetic and

Sophisticated. The more of each of these vitamins and minerals that are provided by each applicant hired/ingested by the organization, the healthier the organization's diet.

In addition to quality of intake, the healthy person/organization also monitors their quantity of intake. Individuals count calories, protein, carbs, fats, sugar, salt, fiber and the resulting impact on waist size, bicep size, dress size and body fat percentages. Comparably, organizations count and try to maximize the ratio of employees required, resources needed, and/or budget allocated to amount of widgets produced.

Exercise

We nurture and develop our bodies by exercising or "training" and then counting improved performance. An organization nurtures its development and improved performance in the same way.

The most effective personal "training" programs are those that have been carefully, professionally developed. Likewise, quality organizations make a priority of developing and utilizing their own unique "training" programs.

Quality organizational training materials begin with some key elements:

- **Key Words and Phrases**–Every organization has a language of its own; jargon, slang, idioms, legalese that is difficult for newcomers to understand. Training materials should include a glossary of such terms so that new employees can become conversant in their new language as quickly as possible.

- **Key Forms**–Explain the purpose of key forms, how to fill out each form, and what to do with it once it's filled out.

- **Key Functions**–Explain the purpose of key functions, and step-by-step directions in simple, plain language on how to perform each function.

- **Key Computer Programs**–Explain the most fundamental, essential computer screens, programs, functions and reports.

- **Key Customer Questions and Requests**–Explain how to respond to the most common questions and requests, whether they come through the mail, e-mail, fax, telephones or across the counter.

- **Key Deadlines, Fees, Laws, Reports, Rules**–Explain any of these elements that are critical to the organization.

Cross-Referencing—Identify important relationships across categories, such as having to be familiar with a particular computer program in order to answer a common customer question, understanding the jargon that is used to categorize data in a report, or knowing that a particular form must be filled out by a deadline.

> **Note:** One organization has had great success hiring school teachers during the summer to develop and/or update training materials. Teachers that do a good job are invited back every summer so that their own growing familiarity and knowledge can be contributed toward the constant improvement of the manual.

> **Note:** One organization has developed a training "University," complete with courses, majors and framed diplomas.

In addition to "training", a second fundamental element of an effective exercise program is counting. It is amazing to observe the degree to which behavior is motivated by counting. We want to climb the "tallest" mountains, wear a certain dress "size", score more "points" than the other team, and make more "money" than the next organization. Numbers are the symbols that allow us to more easily set goals, understand our mission or strive for a result that we can understand. In short:

COUNTING FOCUSES MOTIVATION

REAL LIFE

I once supervised three clerks who made certified copies of legal documents for a fee of $1.00 per page. I knew that one of the three was goofing off and that annual formal review time was approaching. In preparation, for a two-week period I went through their daily receipts and recorded their fees generated. The offender's fees averaged a third of the fees produced by each of the other two. When the offender angrily attacked me over the unfairness of her low review, I calmly showed her my two-week study and asked her if she could explain it, or if she had any other comments or questions. She did not. Counting Focuses Motivation.

REAL LIFE

When I first assumed my current position, there was rampant tardiness and absenteeism. I asked the time and attendance recorder for an account of every employee's status. For those few who had an excellent record, I wrote them a "thank you" note. For the many who had a bad record, I sent them an "informational" note that they had used most of their allotted time and that they might begin working to build it back up in case they ever really needed it. In the next year the number of absenteeism abusers dropped from 44 to 11; and I received numerous "thank yous" from the employees who got appreciation letters. Counting Focuses Motivation.

REAL LIFE

In order to emphasize a priority on quality customer service, I began giving tokens of appreciation (bubble bath, peanuts, microwave popcorn, bags of candy) to employees who received a letter of appreciation from customers for their quality service. During the first two months I gave three each month. Since then, the staff has averaged twenty per month. Counting Focuses Motivation.

REAL LIFE

I supervise ten office sites. Each office files monthly productivity reports. Recently, one of the office managers filed a grievance because she was unhappy with her annual raise. I produced the monthly productivity reports for the previous year, revealing that the highest her office had ranked was seventh and that her average monthly ranking was ninth. I then asked her to explain why she felt that she needed more of a raise. Counting Focuses Motivation.

A few years ago, we implemented a Performance Bonus Pay program in which we calculated some "B+" performance levels and paid bonus pay to those employees who exceeded the standard. For the first couple of months an average of eleven employees exceeded the standard. As the employees learned that quality performance produced extra pay, the number of employees exceeding the productivity standard has risen from the initial average of eleven to an average of forty. Counting Focuses Motivation.

As the above examples attest, almost anything can be counted: attendance, keystrokes, phone calls answered, forms filled out, widgets produced, or money collected. There is some way to count almost anything that you want to focus motivation on, and nurture improvement in.

Esteem

While a healthy diet and a quality exercise program are each important to your organization's development, the fostering of a healthy self-esteem is probably the most critical element in the nurturing of your organization's growth. Obviously, TAP-ing into CCHI creates the overall environment in which esteem can thrive, but we all know that esteem still must be personalized. We all know of supportive "nurtures" that occur in deprived "natures" and despicable "nurtures" that occur in privileged "natures". The greatest opportunity for maximizing potential occurs in the womb of both.

Promoting a strong sense of worth in your organization involves: 1) developing, 2) encouraging/empowering, 3) constructively disciplining, and 4) rewarding.

Progressive development is accomplished, of course, through the diet and exercise regimens of progressive training monitored by performance measurement which identifies strengths and/or weaknesses that may require further training.

Encouraging/Empowering is a personalized version of TAP-ing into CCHI. Organizational CCHI creates the atmosphere, the "nature" to promote individual maximizing/actualizing. Encouraging/empowering creates the opportunity.

Encouraging/Empowering can be injected into either a group or an individual. Entire Departments can be facilitated to identify, creatively respond to and implement solutions/improvements. Committees can be formed to address specific problems or develop specific projects. Individuals can be offered the challenge of doing the same. If your organization has hired PHACES personalities and professionally trained them, why would the organization then manage them restrictively, condescendingly, or dictatorially? One of the core principles of healthy organizations is decentralized empowerment. The great organizations do not have great managers; they have leaders who have TAP-ed into their PHACES' CCHI and empowered them to make the organization great.

REAL LIFE

Many organizations have an 'Employee Congress' in which employee representatives of departments are empowered to meet with leadership to share ideas on how to achieve the organization's mission

REAL LIFE

One organization gives blue ribbons with gold lettering that say 'Why Not' to employees who make creative suggestions. Many recipients proudly hang them from their In-Out Trays. The ribbon refers to the proverb "Some see things as they are and ask 'Why'? Others dream things that never were and say 'Why Not'!

Healthy organizations perceive disciplinary meetings as opportunities to make the employee aware that some of their performance numbers are unacceptable and to offer additional training, re-assignment, or simply understanding and support in order to help them improve their performance.

Unfortunately, even healthy bodies must occasionally expel impure/unhealthy nutrients or remove tumors/cancers. And so do organizations. And, while the expelling/removal of impurities may sometimes be unpleasant and/or painful, we know that it is necessary in order to make the body/organization healthier.

Just as counting motivates, so does recognizing and rewarding. And, just as trophies and medals motivate and recognize athletes, organizations use rewards/recognition to motivate, recognize and appreciate employees. Recognition is a core element of healthy organizations, in which the leader encourages the PHACES to maximize/actualize, and sincerely expresses recognition and appreciation when they excel/succeed. Recognitions–Appreciations tell the employees that leadership: 1) is watching and counting their performance, 2) appreciates quality performance, and 3) values/recognizes/rewards it.

Some of the more common recognitions/rewards utilized by healthy organizations include:

- Personal

    - Extra 30 minutes for lunch

    - Approved Day Off

    - Served Coffee for a Week

- Phone Answered for a Week
- Thank You Card
- Certificate/Plaque/Trophy
- Personalized Coffee Mug/Mouse Pad
- Books
- Candy/Snacks
- Public
  - Employee of the Month Photo
  - Profile on Bulletin Board
  - Story in Newsletter
  - Movable Monthly Trophy
  - Flowers/Plants
  - Balloons
- Monetary
  - Gift Certificates
  - Baskets
  - Free Parking
  - Week-End Getaway
  - Bonus Performance Pay

One organization has identified different categories of performance (attendance, performance, customer appreciation) and awards different colored stickem stars to employees that achieve a certain standard each month. The employees attach them to their 'I'm a Star' ribbon that is hung proudly from their cubicle.

Suggested Work-Out Reminders

___1. Schedule/meet with the Personnel Director and Department Managers with the goal of enhancing the interview process so that applicants who exhibit necessary job skills and PHACES characteristics can be more successfully identified.

Implement recommendations.

___2. Schedule/meet with the Personnel Director and Department Managers to develop a plan for creating/updating training manuals and the training program. Give your organization some AIR (Assign Implementation Responsibilities).

___3. Second Wind. Meet to review progress on training manuals/ program.

___4. Final Sprint. Meet to review progress on training manuals/ program.

___ 5.　Schedule/meet with Personnel Director, Department Managers and Environmentalist to enhance the counting and recognition/reward program. Give AIR (Assign Implementation Responsibilities).

___ 6.　Second Wind. Update meeting on progress of counting and recognition/reward enhancements.

___ 7.　Final Sprint. Update meeting on progress of counting and recognition/reward enhancements.

Communications

(Ears to Brain to Mouth . . . in that order!)

Just as **Nature** and **Nurture** define who your organization is, **Communication** defines what it does, or doesn't do. Successful execution begins with effective communication. Training is not effective if it is not correct and clear. Service is not service unless it is with a smile.

Communication is critical to human success. Those who listen become more knowledgeable than those who don't. Those who articulate with sophistication are more respected than those who don't. The quality of your organization's ability to communicate is equally the foundation of its success or failure.

We all know organizations that make communication very difficult. You call them and are offered recorded messages with no option of a real person. You write them at a P.O. Box, and address a Department rather than a person. They provide no fax number or e-mail addresses. Their web site provides no method of personal interaction. They have very successfully cut themselves off from any communication. They have sentenced themselves first to communication exile and ultimately to extinction. Many of them are currently multi-billion dollar companies, but they have already sentenced themselves to long-term extinction by making conscious management decisions to not communicate. As soon as a competitor makes a priority of customer communication, these dinosaurs will have met their ice age.

Healthy organizations communicate in the same way that successful humans do: 1) they do a lot of listening and learning, and 2) they speak with knowledge and sophistication.

We are told that the "terrible two's" are caused primarily by the frustration that results when a child's brain can think with an intelligence that exceeds its ability to express; in short, frustration caused by a lack of ability to communicate. Consequently, when your organization's communication skills are infantile, it causes frustration among your managers, employees and customers.

In order to develop your organization's communication skills beyond the "terrible two's" phase and, hopefully, to a level of communication sophistication, your organization needs to implement the Organization Communication Fitness Plan.

Diet

Once you've walked that mile and discovered whether or not you're out of breath, whether or not your legs are strong, how quickly and efficiently your heart rate slows, etc., then you can develop your diet strategy to address your weaknesses. Do you need to enhance your e-mail system? Do you need to develop an IVR system? Is your website bloated; does it need to get back to basics, re-focus and streamline?

Develop a diet that will focus/enhance/maximize your quality of service in all phases of organizational communication.

Exercise

A simple but highly beneficial exercise is to walk a mile; and the simplest, but most beneficial, way to analyze/improve your organization's communication systems is to walk a mile in the shoes of a customer. Interact with your organization and see it as customers do. Create a series of commonly occurring customer scenarios and attempt to interact with your organization as a customer would by e-mail, fax, IVR (Interactive Voice Response), telephone, walk-in, web site or other means of contact. Be served, "get the treatment" that your organization is giving customers. Only then can you truly: 1) experience the quality of service that your organization is providing, both technologically and personally; and 2) develop an understanding and appreciation, from the customer's perspective, of what improvements could and should be made.

Esteem

Make sure that your organization is communicating with and serving customers in the same manner that you would like to be communicated with and served. Be a customer and make sure that your own organization serves you better than any other organization you know. Communicate with others, serve others, and do unto others as you would have them do unto you . . . it's that simple.

Suggested Work-Out Reminders

____1. Create real-life scenarios of the most common and more challenging communications needed/desired by your organization's customers.

____2. Have "volunteer" customers (students, senior citizens, etc.) test how your organization's e-mail, fax, IVR, telephone, walk-in, website, or other communication systems respond to and serve your scenarios.

____ 3.   Again, have "volunteer" customers test how your organization's e-mail, fax, IVR, telephone, walk-in, web-site, or other communication systems respond to/serve your scenarios.

____ 4.   Again, have "volunteer" customers test how your organization's e-mail, fax, IVR, telephone, walk-in, web-site, or other communication systems respond to/serve your scenarios.

____ 5.   Analyze the results of your organization's responsiveness to the "volunteer" customers.

____ 6.   Meet with the relevant managers to discuss your experience/findings regarding the organization's responsiveness to "volunteer" customers; praise successes, improve shortcomings and enhance throughout.

____ 7.   Give AIR (Assign Implementation Responsibilities) to improve communication.

____ 8.   Second wind. Verify progress of implementation of programs to improve communication.

____ 9.   Final Sprint. Finalize implementation of programs to improve communication.

Equipment

(Bones, Muscles, Organs, Infrastructure)

Your organization's equipment is the equivalent of your body's bones and muscles; each are elements of infrastructure. The health, strength and quality of an organization's infrastructure are essential to quality performance. Just as you run better on a healthy leg than a broken one, your organization runs better on a healthy copier than a broken one.

Your organization has numerous organs that are critical to its performance. Primary among them are:

Condos   An organization that provides the correct nature/nurture environment provides not workstations but second homes, not cubicles but condos. A person's condo should be just like their home, comfortable and functional.

Copiers   Are one of those muscles that are expected to provide dependable, tireless reps, much like the heart.

Desk Accessories   Organizers, in/out trays, hanging file folders can significantly improve an organization's performance just as cross-training, arm day/leg day, or weight day/cardio day can maximize a body's infrastructure potential.

Desks and Chairs   The right number, the right size, in good condition.

Filing Systems   Critical to maximizing filing systems is efficient use of space and accessibility.

REAL LIFE

I have seen confidential documents filed on open shelves. I have seen legal-sized documents crammed into letter-sized cabinets. I have seen active documents boxed and shipped to warehouses, creating a serious obstacle and delay to efficient productivity.

REAL LIFE

A Probate court dramatically improved its efficiency by preserving its cases on microfiche rather than microfilm. Probate cases can be active for years and one case's various documents might be preserved across hundreds of cartridges of chronologically filmed microfilm. With microfiche,

fiche cards could be created and preserved for each case; new documents could be filmed onto that specific case's fiche card.

Organizers   Just as condo organizers can enhance efficient utilization of space, departmental organizers can do the same for the efficient and effective coordination of the total organization. One example is the centralized wall rack that provides the supply of the most commonly used forms.

Outlets   Computer, fax, telephone and other electrical outlets should be easily accessible without being obstacles.

Others   There may be other pieces of equipment that are critical to various organizations, such as trucks, forklifts, x-ray machines, etc. Whatever equipment is crucial to your organization should be as healthy, strong and dependable as possible.

Diet

Your organization wants equipment that is moderately challenged (exercised) by the amount of work that will be expected of it. If your organization averages 4,000 copies per month, then you want a copy machine that has a capacity of 5,000 per month. Simply, the organization's intake of equipment potential should be moderately challenged by the exercise repetitions that the organization expects from it.

Exercise

If your bones and muscles are not exercised, they get weak. If they are constantly pushed to their limits, they get stressed and/or break. The same thing happens to office equipment. Just as bones and muscles become their strongest with fairly constant moderately challenging exercise, likewise your office equipment is at its best when receiving fairly constant moderate use.

Esteem

Confidence comes with a sense of health and strength. Your organization has a higher self-esteem when it is confident that its bones and muscles are strong and dependable.

REAL LIFE

There is at least one office that has humanized its equipment. Every item has a name. Some items have been given arms, legs, and/or faces. Occasionally, they speak. Whenever the copier, named "Karaoke", breaks down, the sign on it doesn't say "Broken." It says, "I have a headache." And the time clock at 7:55 a.m. plays "Hi Ho, Hi Ho, it's off to work we go" as everyone clocks in.

You can improve the health of your organization's bones and muscles by implementing the following:

Suggested Work-Out Reminders

____ 1.   Ideally, healthy bodies are given annual check-ups to monitor the health and strength of their infrastructure. Organizations should have the same check-up. Distribute the Annual Check-up Checklist (Appendix G) for Department Managers/Staff to fill out.

____ 2.   Meet with Managers/Staff to analyze/implement the findings of the Annual Check-up Checklist (Appendix G) (AIR–*Assign Implementation Responsibilities*).

____ 3.   Second Wind. Check with the Managers/Staff on how equipment enhancement is progressing.

____ 4.   Final Sprint. Meet with Managers/Staff to finalize upgrades, improvements and enhancements to equipment.

Forms/Signs

(Body Language)

Customers of singles hang-outs enter the doors of the establishment with hope and anticipation that they will receive
inviting, encouraging body language that will lead to a successful interaction. The same can be said about your organization. Customers enter the doors of your organization
with hope and anticipation that they will receive inviting,
encouraging body language that will lead to a successful
interaction.

Just as in singles bars, the first encouraging sign that your
organization can impart is a smile. And the phrase that makes
the heart of every single or customer leap is "Can I help you?"

These encouraging signs, the smile and the eagerness to help should be provided by the organization's staff.

> **Note:** A simple 15-minute stroll through your organization to observe whether your staff is smiling and eagerly, pleasantly serving customers can serve as a clear, direct indicator of the effectiveness of your Nature and Nurture programs, the contentment of the staff, and the degree of their 'buy-in' to the organizational mission and to customer service.

REAL LIFE

When consulting with organizations, I like to ask Managers to take me on a tour of their organization. While on the tour, one of the many indicators that I monitor is how the manager acts around customers and the staff; and how the staff reacts when they see the manager coming. This tells me very quickly and accurately the degree to which the Manager has "personified" and imparted throughout the organization a quality Nature and Nurture program.

In addition to the body language of the staff, the organization itself has a body language with which it sends very clear messages to customers. When you enter the typical Post Office or License Plate office and observe the 20-year-old beige paint and the crumbly, peeling, yellowed signs that say "Urgent–Policy Change" at the top and "Effective July 20, 1969" at the bottom; such organizations are sending very clear body language signals that say "rigor mortis". Likewise, when an organization sends out literature that states "Contact Us" but provides no contact phone numbers, e-mail addresses or web sites; that also sends very clear organizational body language that says "Go away".

REAL LIFE

One of my consulting strategies is to observe the client before introducing myself so that I may analyze them before they know that I'm there and know who I am. In one such instance I entered a very public service directed organization and observed that a 40 yard long public service counter had been barricaded with 6 foot high cubicle panels. I first assumed that either the organization had moved or that I had accidentally entered the back door. I looked for the front of the office or for a sign, but found neither. Finally, I noticed someone go through an opening at one end of the counter. I followed and on the other side of the barricade I found a huge room with a maze of unmarked condos (no names or department plaques/signs).

Eventually I stepped into the condo of what appeared to be a pleasant person and asked directions to the Manager's office. Then, out of curiosity, I asked the worker if I had missed the directions or an office map. The worker replied, "Nope". "So customers just wander around and finally ask for directions just like I have?" "Yep."

That organization's "body language" had just sent me and all its other unfortunate victims/customers a very powerful "I don't care, go away, leave me alone" message.

REAL LIFE

One organization complained that its customers would come to the office an average of 3–4 times before successfully completing a transaction because "they keep forgetting simple instructions." "Well, are the instructions in writing?" "No, verbal." The obvious solution was to develop a menu checklist of the most common instructions so that staff could check appropriate instructions and give customers written reminders of what they needed to do. Customer return visits dropped from 3–4 to 2, frustration and hostility due to long lines was reduced and staff became less stressed, frustrated and hoarse. All these improvements were created by more constructive, effective body language.

REAL LIFE

An inventory of one organization revealed that they used 57 different forms. Analysis of the forms revealed that they all dealt with either instructions in 3 different service areas or appropriate fees. The 57 forms were consolidated into 4 menu checklist forms. Storage space was reduced, inventory of form supply was less of a headache, employees spent less time looking for the right form, and body language was more efficient.

REAL LIFE

To psychologically encourage customers to actually read public information signs, one organization placed the image of a red street STOP sign at the top of their most important/informative signs.

Another organization put their messages on a bright white background and hung them under lighting so that the illumination attracted the customer's attention.

REAL LIFE

One university's class registration process was a known nightmare, not because of poor management, but because of a variety of legitimate campus lay-out, space limitation, legal requirements and technology limitation issues. The university chose to turn their 'lemon' ordeal into a 'lemonade' obstacle course game. They placed 14 sequentially numbered, arrowed, directional signs all over campus, directing registrants through the "Following Instructions—

Life Skills" Course. The university's body language message changed from being a disorganized, inept 'joke' to being a creative 'hip' adventure challenge.

So, what body language is your organization giving off, and how can it be improved? What needs to be done so that your organization's forms/signage: 1) SMILE and 2) send the message "May I Help You."

As usual, a combination of Diet, Exercise and Esteem provides the necessary ingredients of success.

Diet

Ensure that you have the appropriate number of signs and forms. Provide every possible beneficial instruction and service while remaining vigilant to trim duplication, consolidate themes and eliminate out-dated forms and signs.

Exercise

Just as in the Communications Unit, your guiding principle is to 'Walk a Mile in Your Customers' Shoes.' Inventory and analyze your organization's forms from the perspective of both your staff and customers. Can the form be modified to be quicker and easier for your staff to work with? Can it be made more clear and understandable to customers? Walk through the organization and look at signage as a customer would. What should be there that is not. What is unclear? What is out-of-date?

Develop improved or new forms and signs as your analysis dictates.

Print, inventory and implement the new/improved forms. Print and install new signs/remove obsolete signs.

Esteem

The design, image, content and location of your organization's signs are clear, direct body language reflecting your organization's personality. We have already discussed how nothing more than creative, fun registration guidance signs converted a college's total image from 'joke' to 'hip'. The same can be done for your organization.

'Walk a Mile in Your Customers' Shoes,' and determine how your organization's signs can SMILE more and offer more clear, concise, informative direction: 1) Look for how phrasing can be clarified and simplified; 2) Think of how signage can be made more innovative, creative, colorful, fun; 3) Think of how signs can be more skillfully, strategically, creatively located; 4) Remove obsolete signs.

Suggested Work-Out Reminders

____ 1.   Select a Public Relations Director, who will supervise the enhancing of the organization's forms/signage, making sure that the organization's body language imparts eager service with a smile.

____ 2.   Meet with the Public Relations Director and their committee. Create the format/structure for the project: 1) Inventory forms/signs 2) Analyze for consolidation, elimination, clarification, creation, and signage location 3) Design 4) Print 5) Install/Implement the new; remove the obsolete.

____ 3.   Second Wind. Meet with Public Relations Director for detailed presentation on progress of organization's enhanced forms/signage.

____ 4.   Final Sprint. Meet with Public Relations Director to finalize installation/implementation of the organization's forms/signage enhancements.

Audits/Laws/Regulations
(Cholesterol)

Laws (lawyers), regulations/procedures, audits (auditors) are an organization's cholesterol. There are good ones (HDLs) and bad ones (LDLs); and the organization must constantly limit the number of bad ones so that they don't clog the organization's arteries, cut off its circulation and cause its death.

Your organization must constantly attempt to increase its HDL; lawyers, regulations, procedures and auditors that constructively promote structured, professional healthy circulation, metabolism, and production. Constructive HDLs are as valuable as life itself, for they realize that their purpose is to provide supporting structure to your organization's mission.

LDLs are parasites, bent on clogging, obstructing your organization's purpose, and too moronic to realize that they are destroying their own host. It cannot be overstated that the necessity to control LDLs is nothing less than a matter of life and death. Just as in real life, where that high LDL diet slowly sneaks up on your body, gradually choking your circulation, oxygen, metabolism; likewise, given the opportunity, lawyers, auditors, and regulations will slowly, request by request, opinion by opinion, rule by rule, order by order, reduce your organization's ability to function. LDLs are the difference between the business that tells its customers, "We're not allowed to do that," and the business that says, "Whatever you want"; the difference between the organization that doesn't fire totally worthless plaque "because employment laws won't let us," and the agency that does fire them "because they are making the organization unhealthy."

Be aware, be alert, and be aggressive about your organization's HDL and LDL counts. It is nothing less than a matter of life and death.

Diet

Identify and count your organization's professional, constructive, productive healthy HDLs and its ridiculous, moronic obstructive LDLs.

Exercise

Research and Identify: 1) internal rules/procedures, 2) external laws/rules/procedures, 3) lawyers, 4) auditors that are beneficial to and promote professional execution of your organization's mission; while likewise identifying internal and external laws/rules/ procedures/lawyers/auditors that are obstructive to your organization's mission. Lobby, work to replace LDLs with HDLs.

Esteem

Tell HDL lawyers and auditors that they are appreciated. When LDL lawyers and auditors are removed from your organization, thank the responsible parties. When HDL laws/rules/procedures are implemented, or LDL laws/rules/procedures are improved/eliminated, thank the responsible parties.

Suggested Work-Out Reminders

____ 1.   Meet with Managers to identify internal and/or external laws/rules/procedures/lawyers/auditors that are helpful or obstructive to your organization's mission.

____ 2.   Express appreciation to constructive lawyers/auditors and initiators of constructive laws/rules/procedures.

____ 3.   Meet with Managers to strategize how to improve/eliminate obstructive laws/rules/procedures; or how to develop/implement constructive laws/rules/procedures. AIR (Assign Implementation Responsibilities)

____ 4.   Meet with Supervisors of obstructive lawyers/auditors to identify constructive, intelligent, professional lawyers/auditors who will replace them in your organization.

____ 5.   Second Wind. Follow up on progress of efforts to design, promote and implement HDL laws/rules/procedures while reducing LDL laws/rules/procedures. Likewise with HDL-LDL lawyers/auditors.

____ 6.   Final Sprint. Finalize implementation of HDL laws/rules/procedures/lawyers/auditors while reducing the number of LDL laws/rules/procedures/lawyers/auditors.

Relationships

(Required, Desired)

It is well documented that sick/old/infirm people exhibit improved health/spirit/will if they are provided relationships, whether with other adults or children, or even animals. Infants are healthier, grow and learn faster if they are given constructive, loving "quality" time. In short, people are happier and healthier when stimulated by relationships.

So is your organization. Healthy, constructive, progressive relationships are critical to an organization's quality of life, its emotional and physical health. Constructive, cooperative, respectful relationships provide the opportunity to partner, to pool resources and skills toward a common goal.

Supportive relationships reinforce esteem and confidence. Friendly competition focuses and motivates.

Human lives are profoundly impacted by the relationships that are beyond our choice: parents, teachers, coaches, bosses. Was a parent an abuser? Did a teacher make math interesting? Did a coach teach a little basketball and a lot of commitment to personal excellence? Our lives are profoundly impacted by unchosen relationships, both good and bad.

We also impact our lives with the relationships that we choose. Do we choose challenging or easy professors, coaches that are spittin-scratchin jocks or teacher-philosophers that use sports as a life lesson, intimate partners that are healthy and supportive, or destructive? These relationship decisions also profoundly affect our lives.

Organizations are just as influenced/impacted by their required and desired relationships. And, as with human relationships, your organization's goal is to minimize stressful/hostile relationships while soliciting/promoting/maximizing positive constructive relationships.

Diet

Research and identify your organization's required relationships as well as the specific functions/demands/responsibilities mandated by the relationship.

Likewise, research and identify desired relationships that could be symbiotic.

Relative to required relationships, conduct process analysis to determine how to streamline and enhance the interaction/relationship.

Relative to potential mutually beneficial symbiotic relationships, document the streamlining/enhancing benefits of the relationship.

Exercise

Work toward implementing the desired modifications/ enhancements, toward developing beneficial new relationships, and toward implementing the potentially beneficial aspects of that relationship.

Esteem

Two commonly known proverbs for the establishment and successful maintenance of relationships are: 1) listen to and respect the other party's needs, and 2) it's amazing what you can accomplish if you are sincerely motivated to achieve the goal itself and don't care anything about who seeks, or receives, recognition for the achievement.

Your esteem, your sense of accomplishment should come

from having improved your organization through developing healthy relationships and making them more positive, efficient, healthy. You will find that your potential partners will be more excited about investing in the relationship if you exhibit that you are equally concerned about their health.

Just as we are more motivated to remain dedicated to a fitness program if we are doing it with others, or if others are constantly enhancing our esteem by noticing and commenting on our progress, so other organizations will be more motivated to cooperate constructively with you if you exhibit that you are sincerely as concerned about their organization's health as you are about your own.

REAL LIFE

An agency wanted to install security plexiglass across its public counters to enhance the perception of security, and reduce lobby noise in the work area. It offered glass businesses a charitable gift letter for tax deduction of the value of contributed glass as well as the right to place an advertising sticker on the glass that was contributed. A glass company responded. It got its tax deduction and advertising, and the agency got its counter glass.

An agency that often had customer lines with wait times of 15–30 minutes worked with a local college's Theatre Dept. to develop an entertaining, informational video for customers to watch, and learn from, while they waited.

Many agencies sell advertising on their web sites to offset the cost of web site maintenance.

Suggested Work-Out Reminders

____ 1.   Distribute to Managers the Organization's Relationship Compatibility Checklist (Appendix H)

____ 2.   Collect and Analyze the responses to the Relationship Compatibility Checklist (Appendix H).

____ 3.   Visit with the Managers to clarify, verify, elaborate on and enhance their responses to the Relationship Compatibility Checklist (Appendix H).

____ 4.   Prioritize responses and develop a plan for implementation of suggestions to enhance relationships.

____ 5.   Seek Managers' suggestions and support for the prioritized plan to enhance relationships.

___ 6. Give your organization AIR (Assign Implementation Responsibilities) to enhance relationships.

___ 7. Second Wind. Update progress on the projects to enhance relationships.

___ 8. Final Sprint. Update progress on implementation and impact of those projects that have been implemented to enhance relationships.

Space

(Joints, Comfortable Contact)

As the human body evolves through life, its physical dimensions change. Babies' heads are disproportionately large, and then the body catches up. Adolescent boys' feet explode into boat paddles. Girls become women. In middle age, gravity pulls everything south. In old age, we shrivel and shrink. Percentage of body fat, height to weight ratios, lung capacity, proper spacing for our discs, proper shape and spacing of our teeth are examples of the importance of healthy spacing within our body.

It is also important that organisms have healthy external spacing. Jogging shoes must provide a snug contour, or can damage our feet. Trees grow the fastest when they touch, grow with, compete with, but are not crowded by other trees. Mice exhibit similar behavior. They are healthiest not when alone or overcrowded, but when in comfortable proximity to other mice, when in a team, a family.

An organism is healthiest when its internal parts are properly spaced and when its external spatial environment is one of comfortable contact. And so it is with your organization. Just as you change your clothes and shoes throughout life to acknowledge and reflect your body's evolutionary changes, so you must occasionally re-organize the spacing within your organization to reflect its evolution. Demand for certain functions may increase or decrease. Changes in laws or in technology may impact resource allocation and space needs.

Consequently, you should occasionally observe or anticipate and plan for the appropriate spacing of your organization's parts; filling in areas where resources/staff have decreased while creating more room for growth areas.

Allocation of space should consider not only adequate physical spacing, but also comfortable psychological spacing. A family unit, a department, should have all of its members together. Staff, trainers, managers, computers, equipment and any symbiotic departments/resources should be placed as conveniently to each other as possible.

Just as an increase in the amount of space taken up by fat, phlegm, plaque and cholesterol is a bad sign for a body, so an increase in the amount of space taken up by badly managed departments, lawyers and accountants/auditors is a bad indicator for an organization. Just as a healthy person tries to keep their fat, phlegm, plaque and cholesterol counts down, so a healthy organization constantly controls the amount of resources and space that is taken up by poorly managed departments, lawyers and auditors.

Diet

Create a Sanitation Department, whose purpose is to dispose of broken, out-dated, un-used equipment and records. Just as your body disposes of waste, it is imperative that your organization also purge waste, creating space for healthy, contributing nutrients.

Exercise

Walk through the organization with Department managers and research space needs, including where space is abundant or cramped, and where family units need to be brought closer together.

Also discuss with Managers their anticipated space needs over the next 5 years, considering production, legal, technological and other factors.

While touring, stay alert to space allocated for lawyers and auditors, and to departments of the organization that are producing more with less, or are asking for more space and resources for no increased production. These are all indicators of health and/or decay.

Make needed physical moves that are targeted to maximize space allocation and bring symbiotic family units closer together.

Esteem

Providing comfortable work space, removing waste, and providing family units easy access to each other all contribute to a healthy image, streamlined productivity, and an atmosphere of structured, organized achievement.

REAL LIFE

An Organization Fitness Trainer (O.F.T.) was working with an Organization which felt that it had an identity and esteem problem. The Organization was made up of a staff of twenty-five in one large room. The O.F.T. observed that the room was arranged so that the telephone staff of six was placed in the center of the room, while the product staff was crammed around the wall. Not only was the spatial psychological message that the telephone staff was most important and production was an afterthought, but the noise created by the telephone staffs' conversations (the Telephone Staff did not have cubicles, they were at open desks) made it difficult for production staff to concentrate.

The O.F.T. proposed re-arranging the entire room, granting the majority of the room to Production, moving the Telephone Unit to one corner and surrounding them with sound absorbing cubicles. Almost immediately the production staff began to develop teamwork, and a sense of mission and pride; inspired by nothing more than a spatial re-organization.

Suggested Work-Out Reminders

____ 1. Send a memo to Dept. Managers, urging them to analyze space needs for the next five years, anticipating production, legal, technology and other potential impacts.

____ 2. Tour physical facilities with Managers, and discuss their 5-year space program vision.

____ 3. Conduct a meeting of all managers to share and coordinate their analyses of space needs. Form consensus on accuracy of analysis, where expansion/retraction is legitimate, how efficient symbioses can be enhanced, and what can be expelled. Give AIR (Assign Implementation Responsibilities).

____ 4. Select a Sanitation Director, whose responsibility is to dispose of/archive/sell/donate obsolete waste. Note: Choose an organized, obsessive-compulsive. They'll love it.

____ 5.   Second Wind. Follow up with Dept. Managers and Sanitation Director on implementation progress of the Space Enhancement project.

____ 6.   Final Sprint. Assist Managers/Sanitation Director toward completion of implementation of the Space Enhancement project.

Supplies

(Vitamins, Supplements)

Years ago, I decided to begin taking vitamins and supplements to enhance my health. As I researched the various vitamins, supplements, and their particular benefits, I was surprised to learn that there was a debate over whether vitamins/supplements actually provided any benefits. I decided to take some for a while and see if I could actually observe any benefits.

Certainly, everyone's metabolism responds differently, but I have noticed a significant increase in the growth and health of my hair and nails when I take Vitamin E, and a significant increase in my body's stamina and gusto during workouts when I eat a health bar about an hour before working out. Consequently, I have come to believe that when taken at the proper time and in the right amounts, vitamins and supplements are beneficial to an organism's health

Of course, the same applies to organizations; and I have come to view office supplies (pens, pencils, magic markers, copier paper, printer cartridges, post-its, etc.) as the equivalent of an organization's vitamins and supplements. They tend to be small, often an afterthought, considered a secondary (supplemental) factor to health. But, when selected and utilized in a managed, structured regimen, they can provide a great benefit to the health and overall well being of an organization.

Just as many health conscious individuals and athletes seek the guidance of nutritionists to develop an appropriate regimen of vitamins/supplements for themselves, so you should select a nutritionist to be responsible for maintaining your organization's supply of healthy supplements.

> **Note:** The impact of a well-managed nutrition program can enhance your organization psychologically as well as physically. Not only does having a constant supply of copier paper readily available keep your organization physically functioning efficiently, but having an organized, dependable, and efficient supply of nutrients serves as one more way

of sending the psychological message that this organization is healthy and hitting on every cylinder.

Diet

Research a healthy intake level of supplies for your organization. What quantity of red pens, blue pens, green magic markers, printer cartridges, printer paper, etc., does your organization need in order to operate efficiently each month?

Expel old, out-dated, dried, faded supplies.

Exercise

Calendar and maintain a healthy stock of vitamins and supplements in the organization's Health Food Store.

Esteem

Keep the Health Food Store clean, shiny, stocked, organized, and available.

Suggested Work-Out Reminders

____ 1.   Appoint an Organizational Nutritionist. Similarly to the selection of the Sanitation Director, choose a personable perfectionist who will combine organization with service.

____ 2.	With the Nutritionist, choose a convenient, accessible location for the Health Food Store.

____ 3.	Assign the Nutritionist to research appropriate, efficient monthly usage levels of various organizational supplies.

____ 4.	Assign the Nutritionist to review current supplies and dispose of old, out-dated useless ones.

____ 5.	Assign the Nutritionist to clean up and organize the 'new' Health Food Store.

____ 6.	Assign the Nutritionist to calendar, maintain and provide supplies, as needed, to the organization.

____ 7.	After a few months, conduct quality control with managers regarding any problems with supply availability and delivery.

____ 8.	After several months, ask the Nutritionist to give you a spur of the moment tour of the Health Food Store so that you can verify that it continues to be clean and organized.

Technology

(Brains/Nervous System)

THE ALERT ORGANIZATION

In my comparison of performance measures among similar organizations, and my analysis of why some organizations are so much more efficient and healthy than others, the elements of success that appear the most often and that have the largest positive impact on an organization's health and performance are the same as the most constructive influences on people: a healthy, constructive, positive, nurturing environment (which we have already discussed) and a healthy, alert, inquisitive, creative, positive brain.

In my studies of those organizations that far surpass their competitors in performance, it amazes me how often I find that the root cause of the superior performance is some technological enhancement that was inspired, incubated, and cultivated by a positive, creative, progressive environment.

Just as with people, organizations that make a priority of brainpower; that stress constant learning, intellectual growth, curiosity, creativity, analysis, synthesis, problem solving, etc., are exercising their brain "muscle", and keeping it faster, stronger, more flexible and healthier than lazy, lethargic brains.

It is imperative to remember that having a physically large brain is not enough; you must use it. And it is not enough to use your brain to think great thoughts in isolation, to be an idea island; you must implement and share those ideas. This implementation and sharing requires a healthy nervous system that has the ability to relay thoughts from the brain to the rest of the body and then to others; the ability to think, act, motivate and empower.

So, your organization's brain is more than a large computer mainframe that has millions of gigabytes of memory. Such organizations may win 'Jeopardy', but not accomplish much else.

Truly successful organizations, like successful, healthy people, are constantly monitoring, developing, enhancing three critical elements of their brain/nervous system:

· Curiosity for relevant (current, beneficial) information

- creative, progressive application

- quick reflexes (action/re-action)

They are mentally, neurologically and reflexively alert (Appendix 1).

REAL LIFE

I once read of a young man who was trying to find business/financial support for an invention. He wrote letters to over fifty businesses that he felt might be interested. He received only one response, from a famous billionaire that he had not even approached. At an international conference the billionaire had overheard one of the targeted businessmen making fun of the young man and his invention. Even though the invention was not relevant to the billionaire's business, he called the young man, they formed a partnership, and were soon selling the invention to the fifty businesses that had not responded. The billionaire and his organization had exhibited how they had become successful; by being alert, by being curious about new opportunities, and by quickly acting on them.

REAL LIFE

Several years ago, there was a major airplane crash at my hometown airport. The news scrolled across the bottom of the television channel that I was watching. I left that channel on for about fifteen more minutes, waiting for a live report, which never came. Finally, I flipped the channel to the news station that was well known to be the best news organization in the community, having won several national awards for quality local news. Sure enough, as I flipped the channel, there was a reporter and camera person hovering over the crash site in a helicopter while a studio reporter was reading the latest press release from the airport. That news organization was "alert." They were a healthy organization whose human and technological brainpower were "alert", able to mobilize, react and respond to the unexpected much more quickly than their competition.

Diet

Make sure that your organization's human and technological brainpower is lean and mean. One creative, motivated innovator is worth more to your organization than ten zombots. Identifying, prioritizing and obtaining, as you can afford to, cutting edge technology or systems that quicken action/reaction dexterity is much healthier to your organization's diet than wasting resources on maintaining slow, lethargic systems. (Note: Anytime that your strategy/goal is to 'maintain' rather than to 'progress', you should thoroughly reconsider your strategy to ensure that it is the best approach.)

Exercise

You should constantly exercise the brains of both your humans and your machines.

There is one leader who constantly buys cross word puzzles, mensa quizzes, and brain teasers for his staff, both to provide them with mental exercises and to send the message that mental dexterity is a priority.

Another leader does something similar with technology. He will occasionally ask his technology staff to produce some new and different report, or perform some new function. If they cannot respond or respond too slowly, he informs them of vendors that can successfully perform that function or, worse, competition that is performing it. Message sent.

In short, constantly exercise; constantly challenge those human and technological brain muscles.

Esteem

Nothing strengthens self-esteem more than positive, constructive nurturing and mental self-confidence. A "smart" organization continues to be curious; it creates, implements and takes pride in new innovations and has confidence that it is alert to and prepared for the unexpected.

Suggested Work-Out Reminders

____ 1. Begin the habit of perusing magazines in your profession, looking for technological developments of others that you might apply or enhance, or new innovations for which you can devise a beneficial adaptation.

____ 2. Distribute a questionnaire to Managers/Staff, requesting their suggestions for technological developments/enhancements.

____ 3. Combine the technological recommendations of Managers/Staff with your own opinions/observations of your organization's specific weaknesses. Identify organizations/vendors that are recognized for being technologically sophisticated in those areas where your organization needs to be strengthened.

____ 4. From this variety of sources (Mags/Journals, Management/Staff Survey, Personal Analysis, Comparison to others), compile a Brain/Nervous System enhancement 'To Do' List.

____ 5. Compile a list of desired programmers/vendors who can provide the most progressive technological solutions to the Brain/Nervous System 'To Do' List.

____ 6. Conduct meetings with programmers/vendors, attended by Managers/Staff Representatives. Identify items on the Brain/Nervous System 'To Do' List that can be done.

Identify related beneficial suggestions recommended by programmers/vendors. Give AIR (Assign Implementation Responsibilities).

____ 7. Meet with Sanitation Director/Managers/Staff Reps. to identify records-files-documents (computer and paper) that can and should be discarded. Assign the task of disposal to the Sanitation Director.

____ 8. Meet with Managers/Staff Reps. to identify data-information-informational resources that require easier access. Identify potential sources of that information (web sites, reference books, reports, universities, etc.). Give AIR to create access to that information for the organization.

____ 9. Second Wind. Check on progress of the Brain/Nervous System 'To Do' List, Disposal of Data Project and Access To Data Project.

____ 10. Final Sprint. Check on progress of the Brain/Nervous System 'To Do' List, The Data Disposal Project, and the Access to Data Project.

Additional Opportunities

(Creating Revelations)

Common sense tells us that a commitment to a healthy lifestyle will be more effective if it is designed so that it becomes a seamless part of our daily routine. This 12-Step Fitness Plan for your organization has been designed so that it can become a routine part of the daily activities of your organization.

While a seamless routine is one key element of a successful healthy lifestyle, it is equally important to introduce an occasional infusion of the unexpected into any long-term commitment. Routine alone may be effective, but it becomes boring, causing interest to fade and commitment to become difficult. Long-term commitment must be fueled by occasional variety and by the anticipation that unexpected fun and surprises are possible.

Just because you normally work-out from 6–7 p.m. doesn't mean that you shouldn't get up on a beautiful fall morning and go for a jog through the crisp fallen leaves, or get on a treadmill or exercycle while you watch your favorite television show at 9:00 p.m. Why just go to the same three restaurants because they have healthy items on the menu? Go to any restaurant of interest and challenge yourself to order a reasonably healthy meal from their menu. Or learn to cook healthy variations of unhealthy dishes that you enjoy.

In short, be committed, not only to developing a healthy lifestyle routine, but to enjoying the creative challenge of finding new healthy variations to it.

You should do the same with this Health and Fitness Lifestyle Plan for your organization. Not only should you be committed to the 10 specific plans already suggested, but you should also constantly search for new ways that your organization's fitness can be improved that do not fit neatly into any of the already discussed categories.

And, just as you initiate and are constantly alert to ideas to enliven your personal lifestyle, so you should initiate, seek out, search for inspirations to improve your organization's health. There are a myriad of potential creativity triggers. One has come to be known as the Adrenalin Rush (Appendix J). We all know that we are often our most creative when we are inspired, excited. Studies show that a key attribute of more creative people is that they retain more of a child-like excitement than most people. The Adrenalin Rush helps trigger that excitement, inspiration, urgency. The Rush identifies some of the most fruitful places to look for ideas on what needs to be done to improve your organization. The list urges you to analyze:

- where organizational backlogs exist,

- where deadlines are missed,

- where customer complaints occur most often,

- what specific employee complaints occur most often,

- where employee turnover occurs most often,

- how the efficiency of high resource use areas in your organization could be improved,

- how the high volume areas in your organization could be streamlined/sped up,

- what ideas/suggestions related to these specific triggers your managers/staff might have, or any other insight they might have,

- where your organization has

poor comparative performance
measures and why, and

- literature that shares the latest
insights and innovations.

But this Rush is just a beginning. The opportunities for inspirations are as limitless as life itself. If Newton could be inspired by an apple falling on his head, who knows what incident in your life might inspire an "ah-hah" moment to the benefit of your organization's health.

REAL LIFE

The leader of one organization that had earned several national recognitions was driving through a small town and noticed all of the local high school's athletic honors proudly displayed on the water tower. "Ah-hah." The leader began displaying the organization's honors on the masthead of the organization's newsletter, reminding everyone that the organization was committed to, and often achieved, excellence.

REAL LIFE

A Department Manager was driving home from a Church Committee meeting where they had discussed ideas for the holiday season (primarily whether to bring live animals into the sanctuary for the presentation of the Nativity scene). But, as the Manager was driving home, she reflected on another suggestion, that Holiday Scent Potpourri be placed around the sanctuary to include the olfactory senses in the holiday season experience. "Ah-hah." The Manager thought that her department's most hectic month of the year was coming up, and if she brought 'peppy' potpourri and candles into the office, they could provide an olfactory pick-me-up to the stressed, beleaguered staff. The staff was surprised, touched and motivated.

REAL LIFE

One leader has developed the habit of jotting down ideas for organizational improvement (his own or those of others) on the last day of the current month on his desk calendar. Then, on that last day of each month, he reviews, analyzes, and reflects on each suggestion, then decides what action to take (forget it, pursue immediate implementation, decide an appropriate future date for implementation and note that designated date and action on his calendar).

> **Note:** Throughout this book, a recurring recommendation has been to have meetings to promote communication, to solicit the wisdom, perspectives and suggestions of others, and to emphasize

the priority that is being placed on progress. Obviously, just as you are striving to make the organization more efficient, you should also make sure that meetings are not just excuses to drink coffee and chit-chat, but that they truly create progress. The obvious way to measure success is to maintain an informal record of the suggestions, insights, cooperations, problems solved, clarifications and other benefits that are produced in the meetings. A more casual, fun way to measure the true benefit of a meeting is to play 'meeting bingo.' Appendix K provides 2 bingo cards. The Quality Meeting Card includes words and phrases that you will hear used in meetings that are sincerely focused on problem solving. The P.C. card contains words and phrases used in meetings that are only interested in giving the appearance of commitment to progress. By noting how many words on each card are used in the meeting (and by which people) you can humorously, insightfully measure the degree of commitment in the meeting to legitimate progress.

Diet

Use the Adrenalin Rush and other inspirations to intake quality suggestions for improvement.

Exercise

Implement quality suggestions.

Esteem

1) By focusing constructively on your flaws and improving them, you enhance esteem. 2) Likewise, by creating an atmosphere of commitment, innovation, creativity, and progress, you instill the psychological adrenalin of the possibility of the unexpected, of surprises, of progress.

Suggested Work-Out Reminders

____ 1.   Give your organization an Adrenalin Rush (Appendix J). Use the creative thought triggers in the 'Rush' to stimulate new ideas (yours, Managers, Staff) for improving your organization's fitness. Give AIR (Assign Implementation Responsibilities).

____ 2.   Establish one day per month that you can allocate some time to thinking of, analyzing, implementing and monitoring new ideas for improving your organization's fitness. Blend them in with Adrenalin Rush inspirations.

_____ 3.   Second Wind. Monitor the progress of implementation of ideas inspired by an Adrenalin Rush.

_____ 4.   Final Sprint. Encourage final implementation of ideas inspired by an Adrenalin Rush.

_____ 5.   Stay alert. Stay alive. Keep senses alert. Truly live today as if it may be your last, and your organization's. Be positively, constructively joyful.

Rest, Reflect, Meditate

(Cool down, meditation, sleep)

Active organisms must rest. They must have down time, rest physically, reflect on what they have recently accomplished, and meditate on what they need to do and where they need to go next.

Rest, reflection and meditation keep progress organized and planned rather than haphazard and frenetic.

Rest, reflection and meditation make progress sustainable and replenishable, rather than a short term fad that burns out.

Rest, reflection and meditation keep progress refreshed and energized rather than mentally and physically tired.

A mentally and physically rested organism is alert for and excited about the next opportunity to improve.

Rest: Take a day off. Sleep late. Take a walk in the woods. Go to a movie. Go out to eat and have dessert.

Reflect: Think about the organization's accomplishments. Remind yourself of where the organization used to be and how it has improved. Think of improvements that have been made in staff quality, projects completed, performance measurement improvements. Remind yourself that the organization has made a lot of progress to be proud of.

Meditate: Focus on the Unfinished, the Unresolved and the Unknown.

Compile a mental organized list of the current status of unfinished projects and what obstacles remain to their successful completion.

Compile a mental organized list of problems, issues, obstacles, and weaknesses that have arisen and are not currently being addressed.

Think a bit about the future. Try to anticipate problems, issues, obstacles, and weaknesses that lurk just beyond the horizon.

Don't try to grapple with these issues today. Wait to do that at the office. Remember, you're resting! Today, you're not struggling with problems; you're creating an environment where you can calmly, pleasantly, casually think, reflect, and meditate. In this atmosphere you will be able to more thoroughly and accurately anticipate the future, identify current issues, and appreciate your accomplishments.

And, today, that's all you're doing!

Suggested Work-Out Reminders

____ 1.   Take a day off. Get away, where you can calmly, pleasantly, casually think, reflect, meditate.

- Anticipate the unknown.

- Identify the unresolved.

- Update the status of current projects.

- Appreciate the organization's accomplishments.

____ 2.   In mid-December, go shopping. Spend a day getting Holiday gifts for Managers and Departments. Personal or Inspirational gifts work well for Managers. Popcorn, candles, fruit baskets, candy canes, pastries work well for Departments.

____ 3.   In the last week of December, compile a list of unfinished projects and issues that need to be addressed at the early January Managers' meeting where next year's Organization Improvements plan is developed.

____ 4.   In the last week of December, compile a list of the year's organizational accomplishments: improved performance measures, projects completed, staff that has dramatically improved, new quality staff hired, technology enhancements, etc. Distribute the list in an end of the year 'Thank You' letter to staff.

____ 5.   Send a copy of your Annual "Thank You" letter and/or 'Weigh In' Form to me at:

Fit For Service

1101 Churchill

Irving, Texas 75060

Or:

www.fitforservice.org

Or:

fitforservice@Verizon.net

Let me know how the Actualized Organization Fitness Plan has helped your organization.

To Your Organization's Health…

I used to live close to a high school that had a track around its football field. Each January 2, 3, and 4, I would drive by the track on my way home each afternoon and see 40 to 50 people plodding around, struggling with their New Year's resolution to "get in shape." By mid January, within two weeks, they were all gone.

Several years ago a major corporation ran an ad campaign called "50 Reasons Not to Change," and listed 50 phrases and excuses that are used by those avoiding or obstructing progress.

The vast majority of people and organizations may occasionally have short-term good intentions; but generally succumb to long-term bad habits. It is the rare person (or organization) that realizes that good health and maximizing their potential cannot be achieved by grudgingly making themselves allocate thirty minutes to an hour a day to the task; but by making a positive, joyful lifestyle commitment to excellence that reaps the benefit of mental, physical, and emotional excellence every day.

The 12-Step Fitness Plan for your Organization will transform it into one of the few mentally, physically, emotionally fit and happy organizations in existence.

Three years from now, you will be amazed at how much more efficient your organization is, at how much money you are saving on expenses, at how much more you are keeping in profits, at how much good you are achieving in the world by allocating some of those savings/profits to philanthropy, at how happy and motivated your staff is, at how often your organization (and you) are admired and praised, at how life itself has become an endorphin charged final sprint.

Start today.

To your organization's health.

For advice or assistance, or to tell me about your organization's accomplishments, progress and philanthropies, contact me at:

Fit For Service
1101 Churchill
Irving, Texas 75060
972–579–8057
www.fitforservice.org
EMAIL: fitforservice@verizon.net

Appendix A

T radition (pride)

A tmosphere (CCHI)

P urpose (mission, goals)

into your organization's

C ivility

C reativity

H umanity

I ntegrity

Appendix B

PHACES

Interview Analysis Sheet

POSITIVE

Negative		Positive
Defeatist		Constructive
Can't Do		Let's Do

Comments: _____

HAPPY

Unhappy		Happy
Pessimistic		Humorous
Complainer		
Blamer		

Comments: _____

ALERT

Lethargic		Attentive
Inattentive		Focused
Distracted		

Comments: _____

CONFIDENT

Insecure   Confident

Fearful   Relaxed

Arrogant   Understated

    Comments: _____

ENERGETIC

Listless   Motivated

Discouraged   Purposeful

Hyper   Enthusiastic

Distracted

    Comments: _____

SOPHISTICATED

Poor Communication   Fluent

Flawed Thought   Sound Reasoning

Crude Demeanor   Civility

    Comments: _____

Appendix C

"Every word you speak;

Every behavior you exhibit;

Every decision you make;

Personifies the Organization's Commitment to

TAP-ing into its CCHI."

Appendix D

7 Phaces of Growth

Hire

Train

Count

Develop

Encourage/empower

Re-focus

Reward

Appendix E

_____	Key Words And Phrases
_____	Key Forms
_____	Key Functions
_____	Key Computer Programs
_____	Key Customer Questions/requests
_____	Key Deadlines
	Reports
	Laws
	Rules
	Fees
_____	Key Cross-references

Appendix F

Counting

Focuses

Motivation

Appendix G (1)

ANNUAL CHECK-UP CHECKLIST

Existing Equipment	Current Capacity (Too Low/Correct/ Not Fully Utilized)	Dependability (Y/N – Explain)	Location (Ideal/Move to – Explain)

ANNUAL CHECK-UP CHECKLIST

Equipment Needed	Capacity Needed (Slightly more than average projected usage)	Ideal Location (Explain)

APPENDIX H

RELATIONSHIP COMPATIBILITY CHECKLIST

Relationships	Recommendations
Required 1 2	 1 2
Desired 1 2	 1 2
Delays 1 2	 1 2
Duplications 1 2	 1 2
Log-jams 1 2	 1 2

Relationships	Recommendations
Misconnects	
1	1
2	2
Pass The Bucks	
1	1
2	2
Opportunities	
1	1
2	2

Appendix I

THE ALERT ORGANIZATION

Curiosity   for Relevant
                                  Current
                                  Beneficial
                                  Information

Creative   Progressive
                                  Application

Quick   Reflexes

APPENDIX J

THE ADRENALIN RUSH

Adrenalin	Rush/Ideas
Backlogs 1 2	1 2
Customer Complaints 1 2	1 2
Employee Complaints 1 2	1 2
Employee Turnover 1 2	1 2
High Resource Use 1 2	1 2

Adrenalin	Rush/Ideas
High Volume Functions 1 2	1 2
Ideas/Suggestions of Management/Staff 1 2	1 2
Missed Deadlines 1 2	1 2
Poor Comparative Performance Measures 1 2	1 2
Professional Literature 1 2	1 2

Appendix K (1)

P. C. MEETING BINGO

At the End of the Day	Client Focus	Knowledge Base	Pro-active	Take That Off Line
Ball Park	Core Competencies	Leverage	Result Driven	Think Outside the Box
Benchmark	Empower	24/7 OR 110%	Re-visit	Touch Base
Best Practice	Fast Track	Mind Set	Strategic	Value Added
Bottom Line	Game Plan	Out of the Loop	Synergy	Win-win

QUALITY MEETING BINGO

Analyze	Develop	Impact	Plan	Ripple Effect
Compare	Effective	Implement	Positive	Step
Cost Benefit	Efficient	Improve	Progress	Thanks
Creative	Employee	Maximize	Quality	Train
Customer	Follow-up	Performance Measures	Results	Vision/Mission

Appendix L

THE MEDITATION MANTRA

"The Unfinished

The Unresolved

The Unknown"

Appendix M

NATURE: AN ORGANIZATION'S SOUL

(Office Environment)

The Purposeful Family

TAP into CCHI:

- Tradition
- Atmosphere–CCHI (Civility, Creativity, Humanity, Integrity)
- Purpose (Mission, Goals)

Diet

- Quality Intake (Phaces)

Exercise

- Personify

Esteem

- Personnel Director
- Initiation

Suggested Plan

NURTURE

(Development/Growth)

Maximize Resources

Diet

- Intake Phaces
- Vitamins/supplements
- (Enhance/empower)

Exercise

- Training Manual Checklist
- Train
- Count

Esteem

- Develop (Train-count)
- Encourage/Empower
- Constructive Discipline
- Reward

Suggested Plan

(Ears To Brain To Mouth . . . In That Order!)

The Terrible Two's

Communication Sophistication

Exercise

- "Walk A Mile In My Shoes":

    E-mail

    Fax

    IVR

    Phone

    Web

    Other

Diet

- Firm Up

- Enhance

- Maximize

Esteem

- Golden Rule

Suggested Plan

EQUIPMENT

      (Bones, Muscles, Organs, Infrastructures)

Constant, Moderate Resistance

Diet

- Healthy, Functional Size

Exercise

- Constant Moderate Challenge

Esteem

- Dependable
- Location

Suggested Plan

- The Annual Check-up Checklist

FORMS/SIGNS

(Body Language)

"May I Help You"

Diet

- Duplication
- Consolidation
- Elimination

Exercise

- Inventory—"Walk A Mile In My Shoes"
- Analysis
- Develop
- Installation

Esteem

- Clarification
- Creativity
- Presentation

Suggested Plan

(Cholesterol)

Increase Healthy Circulation

Minimize Obstructions

Diet

. Count

Exercise

. Work To Improve

Esteem

. Appreciate

Suggested Plan

(Required, Desired)

Positive, Constructive Relationships

Diet

- Identify
- Develop
- Enhance

Exercise:

- Approach/initiate
- Implement

Esteem:

- Listen
- Sincerely Care
- Give

Suggested Plan:

- Relationship Compatibility Checklist

(Joints, Comfortable Contact)

Internal–efficient, lubricated, comfortable

External–comfortable contact

Healthy utilization of space:

- . Healthy (Bones, Muscles)

     Vs

- . Unhealthy (Cholesterol/phlegm)

Exercise

- . Evaluate
- . Anticipate

Diet

- . Sanitation Dept.
- . Expel

Esteem

- . Organize
- . Re-arrange

Suggested Plan

SUPPLIES

(Vitamins, Supplements)

Nutritionist

Health Food Store

Diet

- Research Healthy Intake
- Expel

Exercise

- Calendar
- Stock
- Maintain

Esteem

- Clean
- Organized

Suggested Plan

TECHNOLOGY

(Brains/Nervous System)

The Alert Organization

Curiosity

Creative Application

Quick Reflexes

Exercise

- Awareness
- Dexterity
- Quickness
- Implementation

Diet

- Discernment

Esteem

- Mental Confidence

Suggested Plan

(Cool Down, Meditation, Sleep)

Rest

Your Favorite Things

Reflect On Accomplishments

Meditate

· The Meditation Mantra

"The Unfinished, The Unresolved, The Unknown"

Appendix N

WEIGH IN

____ 1) Total Budget ÷ Widgets Produced = Cost Per Widget

$_____ ÷ _____ = $_____

____ 2) This Year Cost Per Widget ÷ Last Year Cost Per Widget

= % Efficiency Improvement (% Improved Health)

$_____ ÷ _____ = _____ %

____ 3) % Efficiency Improvement ÷ 10%

= Charitable Contribution %

_____ % ÷ 10% = _____ %

____ 4) Total Budget ÷ Charitable Contribution %

= Charitable Contribution

$_____ ÷ _____ % = $_____

____ 5) Write Check:

Heifer International
1015 Louisiana
Little Rock, Arkansas 72202

____ 6) Tell Us About Your Success:

Fit For Service
1101 Churchill
Irving, Texas 75060
972–579–8057
Www.fitforservice.org
Email: Fitforservice@verizon.net

APPENDIX O

WORK-OUT REMINDERS

CHAPTERS 7-18

Suggested Work-Out Reminders

____ 1.   Select an office Environmentalist. Their function, for lack of a better term, is to be the organization's cheerleader. This person makes sure that things are done to create a positive, prideful atmosphere, that the healthy Purposeful Family environment is maintained, and conditions are maximized for TAP-ing into the organization's CCHI. The Environmentalist will probably want to participate in or supervise some of the following suggestions.

____ 2.   If your organization does not already recognize holidays, special fun days and/or the organization's significant historical events, the Environmentalist may wish to start making such days part of the organization's culture.

- Do you hunt plastic Easter eggs in the office for Easter?
- Do you have best carved pumpkin contests at Halloween?
- Do you have ugliest socks day?
- Do you honor the organization's founder's birthday or the anniversary of the big "breakthrough" contract?

____ 3.   The Environmentalist may wish to form a committee whose purpose is to create, implement and maintain visibility for an organizational logo and mission statement. Both help create a foundation, pride and tradition.

____ 4.   The Environmentalist may create a Tradition Committee to research, record and promote organizational great achievements, historic moments, folklore, Outstanding Employee Hall of Fame, etc.

____ 5.   The Tradition Committee should create, maintain and update a Wall of Tradition.

____ 6.   Produce a bi-monthly or quarterly organizational newsletter. The Newsletter will include:

- The Organization's logo
- Mission Statement
- Recent accomplishments, upgrades, improvements
- Procedure/law changes
- Reminders relative to correcting glitches
- Update on status of efforts to implement office goals

- Update on performance relative to performance standards
- Recognition of employees who have received an appreciation from a customer
- News from departments
- Employee profiles
- Recognition of birthdays, anniversaries, children, promotions, etc.
- Appropriate games, jokes, stories, etc.
- Any other relevant/appropriate contribution.

___ 7. Conduct quarterly meetings with representatives of the employees (The Employees' Congress) so that you can communicate with and learn from them directly.

___ 8. The Environmentalist should design, update and place in each new employee's packet a "Welcome to the Family" letter that includes a brief initiation into Organization history, lore, tradition, achievements and a welcome on becoming a part of it; signed by the Organization's President, the Human Resources Director, the Environmentalist, and the Chairman of the Tradition Committee.

___ 9. As a part of their first day, new hires should be given their "New Employee Packet" that includes not only the required rules, procedures, legal/tax forms, etc., but also the "Welcome to the Family" letter, a copy of the most recent Organization Newsletter, and the training materials for the department that they are assigned to. The Human Resources Director or the Environmentalist should take them on a tour of the Organization completed by a visit to and explanation of the Wall of Tradition.

Chapter 8 – Nurture
(Development/Growth)

Suggested Work-Out Reminders

____ 1. Schedule/meet with the Personnel Director and Department Managers with the goal of enhancing the interview process so that applicants who exhibit necessary job skills and PHACES characteristics can be more successfully identified.

· Implement recommendations.

____ 2. Schedule/meet with the Personnel Director and Department Managers to develop a plan for creating/updating training manuals and the training program. Give your organization some AIR (Assign Implementation Responsibilities).

____ 3. Second Wind. Meet to review progress on training manuals/program.

____ 4. Final Sprint. Meet to review progress on training manuals/program.

____ 5. Schedule/meet with Personnel Director, Department Managers and Environmentalist to enhance the counting and recognition/reward program. Give AIR (Assign Implementation Responsibilities).

____ 6. Second Wind. Update meeting on progress of counting and recognition/reward enhancements.

____ 7. Final Sprint. Update meeting on progress of counting and recognition/reward enhancements.

CHAPTER 9 – COMMUNICATIONS
(Ears to Brain to Mouth . . . in that order!)

Suggested Work-Out Reminders

____ 1. Create real-life scenarios of the most common and more challenging communications needed/desired by your organization's customers.

____ 2. Have "volunteer" customers (students, senior citizens, etc.) test how your organization's e-mail, fax, IVR, telephone, walk-in, website, or other communication systems respond to and serve your scenarios.

____ 3. Again, have "volunteer" customers test how your organization's e-mail, fax, IVR, telephone, walk-in, web-site, or other communication systems respond to/serve your scenarios.

____ 4. Again, have "volunteer" customers test how your organization's e-mail, fax, IVR, telephone, walk-in, web-site, or other communication systems respond to/serve your scenarios.

____ 5. Analyze the results of your organization's responsiveness to the "volunteer" customers.

____ 6. Meet with the relevant managers to discuss your experience/findings regarding the organization's responsiveness to "volunteer" customers; praise successes, improve shortcomings and enhance throughout.

____ 7. Give AIR (Assign Implementation Responsibilities) to improve communication.

____ 8. Second wind. Verify progress of implementation of programs to improve communication.

____ 9. Final Sprint. Finalize implementation of programs to improve communication.

CHAPTER 10 — EQUIPMENT
(Bones, Muscles, Organs, Infrastructures)

Suggested Work-Out Reminders

____ 1.   Ideally, healthy bodies are given annual check-ups to monitor the health and strength of their infrastructure. Organizations should have the same check-up. Distribute the Annual Check-up Checklist (Appendix G) for Department Managers/Staff to fill out.

____ 2.   Meet with Managers/Staff to analyze/implement the findings of the Annual Check-up Checklist (Appendix G) (AIR – Assign Implementation Responsibilities).

____ 3.   Second Wind. Check with the Managers/Staff on how equipment enhancement is progressing.

____ 4.   Final Sprint. Meet with Managers/Staff to finalize upgrades, improvements and enhancements to equipment.

Chapter 11 — Forms/Signs
(Body Language)

Suggested Work-Out Reminders

___ 1.   Select a Public Relations Director, who will supervise the enhancing of the organization's forms/signage, making sure that the organization's body language imparts eager service with a smile.

___ 2.   Meet with the Public Relations Director and their committee. Create the format/structure for the project: 1) Inventory forms/signs 2) Analyze for consolidation, elimination, clarification, creation, and signage location 3) Design 4) Print 5) Install/Implement the new; remove the obsolete.

___ 3.   Second Wind. Meet with Public Relations Director for detailed presentation on progress of organization's enhanced forms/signage.

___ 4.   Final Sprint. Meet with Public Relations Director to finalize installation/implementation of the organization's forms/signage enhancements.

CHAPTER 12—AUDITS/LAWS/REGULATIONS
(Cholesterol)

Suggested Work-Out Reminders

___ 1.　　　Meet with Managers to identify internal and/or external laws/rules/procedures/lawyers/auditors that are helpful or obstructive to your organization's mission.

___ 2.　　　Express appreciation to constructive lawyers/auditors and initiators of constructive laws/rules/procedures.

___ 3.　　　Meet with Managers to strategize how to improve/eliminate obstructive laws/rules/procedures; or how to develop/implement constructive laws/rules/procedures. AIR (Assign Implementation Responsibilities)

___ 4.　　　Meet with Supervisors of obstructive lawyers/auditors to identify constructive, intelligent, professional lawyers/auditors who will replace them in your organization.

___ 5.　　　Second Wind. Follow up on progress of efforts to design, promote and implement HDL laws/rules/procedures while reducing LDL laws/rules/procedures. Likewise with HDL-LDL lawyers/auditors.

___ 6.　　　Final Sprint. Finalize implementation of HDL laws/rules/procedures/lawyers/auditors while reducing the number of LDL laws/rules/procedures/lawyers/auditors.

Chapter 13 — Relationships
(Required, Desired)

Suggested Work-Out Reminders

___ 1.　　Distribute to Managers the Organization's Relationship Compatibility Checklist (Appendix H).

___ 2.　　Collect and Analyze the responses to the Relationship Compatibility Checklist (Appendix H).

___ 3.　　Visit with the Managers to clarify, verify, elaborate on and enhance their responses to the Relationship Compatibility Checklist (Appendix H).

___ 4.　　Prioritize responses and develop a plan for implementation of suggestions to enhance relationships.

___ 5.　　Seek Managers' suggestions and support for the prioritized plan to enhance relationships.

___ 6.　　Give your organization AIR (Assign Implementation Responsibilities) to enhance relationships.

___ 7.　　Second Wind. Update progress on the projects to enhance relationships.

___ 8.　　Final Sprint. Update progress on implementation and impact of those projects that have been implemented to enhance relationships.

Chapter 14 — Space
(Joints, Comfortable Contact)

Suggested Work-Out Reminders

____ 1. Send a memo to Dept. Managers, urging them to analyze space needs for the next five years, anticipating production, legal, technology and other potential impacts.

____ 2. Tour physical facilities with Managers, and discuss their 5-year space program vision.

____ 3. Conduct a meeting of all managers to share and coordinate their analyses of space needs. Form consensus on accuracy of analysis, where expansion/retraction is legitimate, how efficient symbioses can be enhanced, and what can be expelled. Give AIR (Assign Implementation Responsibilities).

____ 4. Select a Sanitation Director, whose responsibility is to dispose of/archive/sell/donate obsolete waste. Note: Choose an organized, obsessive-compulsive. They'll love it.

____ 5. Second Wind. Follow up with Dept. Managers and Sanitation Director on implementation progress of the Space Enhancement project.

____ 6. Final Sprint. Assist Managers/Sanitation Director toward completion of implementation of the Space Enhancement project.

Suggested Work-Out Reminders

____ 1.   Appoint an Organizational Nutritionist. Similarly to the selection of the Sanitation Director, choose a personable perfectionist who will combine organization with service.

____ 2.   With the Nutritionist, choose a convenient, accessible location for the Health Food Store.

____ 3.   Assign the Nutritionist to research appropriate, efficient monthly usage levels of various organizational supplies.

____ 4.   Assign the Nutritionist to review current supplies and dispose of old, out-dated useless ones.

____ 5.   Assign the Nutritionist to clean up and organize the "new" Health Food Store.

____ 6.   Assign the Nutritionist to calendar, maintain and provide supplies, as needed, to the organization.

____ 7.   After a few months, conduct quality control with managers regarding any problems with supply availability and delivery.

____ 8.   After several months, ask the Nutritionist to give you a spur of the moment tour of the Health Food Store so that you can verify that it continues to be clean and organized.

CHAPTER 16 — TECHNOLOGY
(Brains/Nervous System)

Suggested Work-Out Reminders

_____ 1. Begin the habit of perusing magazines in your profession, looking for technological developments of others that you might apply or enhance, or new innovations for which you can devise a beneficial adaptation.

_____ 2. Distribute a questionnaire to Managers/Staff, requesting their suggestions for technological developments/ enhancements.

_____ 3. Combine the technological recommendations of Managers/Staff with your own opinions/observations of your organization's specific weaknesses. Identify organizations/vendors that are recognized for being technologically sophisticated in those areas where your organization needs to be strengthened.

_____ 4. From this variety of sources (Mags/Journals, Management/Staff Survey, Personal Analysis, Comparison to others), compile a Brain/Nervous System enhancement 'To Do' List.

_____ 5. Compile a list of desired programmers/vendors who can provide the most progressive technological solutions to the Brain/Nervous System 'To Do' List.

_____ 6. Conduct meetings with programmers/vendors, attended by Managers/ Staff Representatives. Identify items on the Brain/Nervous System 'To Do' List that can be done. Identify related beneficial suggestions recommended by programmers/vendors. Give AIR (Assign Implementation Responsibilities).

_____ 7. Meet with Sanitation Director/Managers/Staff Reps. to identify records-files-documents (computer and paper) that can and should be discarded. Assign the task of disposal to the Sanitation Director.

_____ 8. Meet with Managers/Staff Reps. to identify data-information-informational resources that require easier access. Identify potential sources of that information (web sites, reference books, reports, universities, etc.). Give AIR to create access to that information for the organization.

_____ 9. Second Wind. Check on progress of the Brain/Nervous System 'To Do' List, Disposal of Data Project and Access To Data Project.

_____ 10. Final Sprint. Check on progress of the Brain/Nervous System 'To Do' List, The Data Disposal Project, and the Access to Data Project.

Chapter 17 — Additional Opportunities
(Creating Revelations)

Suggested Work-Out Reminders

____ 1. Give your organization an Adrenalin Rush (Appendix J). Use the creative thought triggers in the "Rush" to stimulate new ideas (yours, Managers, Staff) for improving your organization's fitness. Give AIR (Assign Implementation Responsibilities).

____ 2. Establish one day per month that you can allocate some time to thinking of, analyzing, implementing and monitoring new ideas for improving your organization's fitness. Blend them in with Adrenalin Rush inspirations.

____ 3. Second Wind. Monitor the progress of implementation of ideas inspired by an Adrenalin Rush.

____ 4. Final Sprint. Encourage final implementation of ideas inspired by an Adrenalin Rush.

____ 5. Stay alert. Stay alive. Keep senses alert. Truly live today as if it may be your last, and your organization's. Be positively, constructively joyful.

Suggested Work-Out Reminders

____ 1.   Take a day off. Get away, where you can calmly, pleasantly, casually think, reflect, meditate.

    · Anticipate the unknown.
    · Identify the unresolved.
    · Update the status of current projects.
    · Appreciate the organization's accomplishments.

____ 2.   In mid-December, go shopping. Spend a day getting Holiday gifts for Managers and Departments. Personal or Inspirational gifts work well for Managers. Popcorn, candles, fruit baskets, candy canes, pastries work well for Departments.

____ 3.   In the last week of December, compile a list of unfinished projects and issues that need to be addressed at the early January Managers' meeting where next year's Organization Improvements plan is developed.

____ 4.   In the last week of December, compile a list of the year's organizational accomplishments: improved performance measures, projects completed, staff that has dramatically improved, new quality staff hired, technology enhancements, etc. Distribute the list in an end of the year "Thank You" letter to staff.

____ 5.   Send a copy of your Annual "Thank You" letter and/or "Weigh In" Form to me at:

Fit For Service

1101 Churchill

Irving, Texas 75060

or:

www.fitforservice.org

or:

fitforservice@Verizon.net

Let me know how the Actualized Organization Fitness Plan has helped your organization.

The "Fit for Service" Mission

"Recycle Inefficiency into Philanthropy"

The Mission of Fit for Service is to "recycle inefficiency into philanthropy." David Childs, Ph.D. explains, "There is immense operational waste in the world's organizations. Clearly, commitment to identify and reduce that waste, then invest it into clean water, basic education, pre-natal care and other wisely targeted methods to dramatically enhance humanity's future. Organizations and humans can create a symbiotic relationship in which each provides the other the opportunity to actualize."

David Childs, Ph.D.

October 4, 1999

ABOUT THE AUTHOR

David Childs, Ph. D. has been Dallas County, Texas Tax Assessor/Collector for 17 years where he has developed and applied the Fit for Service concepts. As a result, the Tax Office has earned 3 State of Texas and 4 national recognitions for quality management, and has been visited by 5 international delegations. Dr. Childs speaks at numerous conferences and seminars, teaches MBA courses in Systems Thinking and in Transformational Leadership, and is an examiner for Texas Quality (Texas' Malcolm Baldrige Award).

Dr. Childs is married to Alice Canham, who is a fund-raiser for the Susan G. Komen Breast Cancer Foundation. Daughter Lauren is majoring in medical research at Ohio State University, and daughter Emily is majoring in literature and creative writing at Mary Hardin Baylor University.